heart

[not hype]

RESTORATION
GENERATION

resgen.org

heart

[not hype]

TOM HENDERSON

THRONE
PUBLISHING GROUP

Book design by Tim Murray, paperbackdesign.com/books

Throne Publishing Group
220 S. Phillips Ave.
Sioux Falls, SD 57104

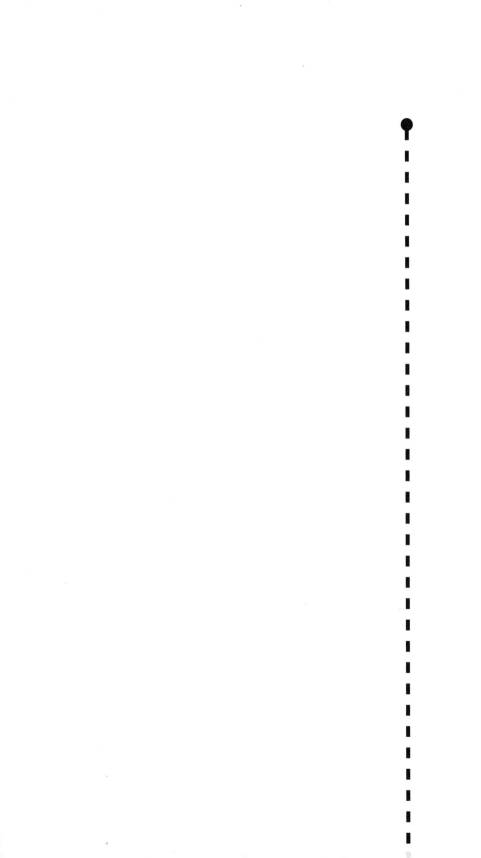

Aaron Countryma

ICC church

Special thanks to:

My Family – Especially my wife Laura, and my boys, Isaiah and Chase-you inspire me to be a better husband, dad and follower of Christ everyday. Thank you for the sacrifices you make daily for me to do what God has called me to do!

My partners in ministry – Your prayer and financial support keep Restoration Generation moving forward in God's call and making an impact for the Kingdom. Thank you for being a constant source of encouragement to us!

LifeLight – Your belief in me as a speaker and evangelist helped launch me into the adventure of a lifetime. Thank you for giving me the opportunity to write and speak while on staff with you.

Tom has really hit the mark with *Heart Not Hype*.
As a student, it is hard to remain fully crazy
for the Lord but through this book I learned
amazing ways to keep God at the center of my
life, whether I am in the darkest valley or on the
highest mountaintop.

Zane, high school student

Tom's passion for following Christ is so evident
throughout *Heart Not Hype*! This book truly
draws you in and needs to be shared with both
believers and non-believers alike. Rock on!

Michelle, high school student

Heart Not Hype is an amazing 7-day experience!
Accepting Christ into your heart is a life
changing decision and this book is full of truth
that will help you along that beautiful journey.

Natalie, high school student

I read the whole book in one day! I know
I wasn't necessarily supposed to but I just
couldn't put it down!

Joe, junior high student

(More responses on page 114)

introduction:
read this first

Wouldn't it be sweet if you could just live your life going from vacation to vacation? Or live inside your favorite action/adventure movie? Or go from one exciting event to the next mountaintop experience? **Sounds pretty good, right?**

As much as we may want to live our lives on the mountaintop...

I remember being a kid and thinking that I was going to grow up to be Luke Duke from the 1980's TV show Dukes of Hazzard (If you haven't heard of that show, you may want to Google it). I was enamored with the idea of actually going through life being him – for real – being Luke Duke. I used to think about being so tough that I could beat up absolutely any bad guy in a brawl (no matter how big and bad they were) and then driving away in the General Lee – my race car that I had to get into by going through the window because the car doors were sealed shut. This car was so tough that it had the ability to jump 50-foot chasms and land with no impact on the vehicle whatsoever. Of course in order to drive this amazing vehicle, I also had the sweetest of driving skills so I could escape the very intimidating officers of the law like Rosco P. Coltrane. As I think back on this though, there was one difference about how things played out in my mind – in the show, Daisy was my cousin, but in my world, she was my girlfriend. Yes, it's true – she was my first TV crush...her and Wonder Woman.

Well anyway, while all of that may sound desirable, unfortunately scenarios like that just aren't reality are they? As much as we may want to live our lives on the mountaintop and experience the excitement of being Luke Duke (or whoever your favorite action hero is) the majority of our days are spent walking in the valleys of challenges and on the plains of normalcy. You know exactly what I am talking about don't you? Sure you do. After all, 99% of the world can't just lie on the beach whenever they want to or snowboard down the mountains of Colorado day in and day out. And most likely, you and I are part of that 99%. Instead, we have to go to school, punch the time clock at work and do our chores at home. We have to meet expectations, pay our bills and take care of our responsibilities. That, my friends, is life. And, no matter how much we want it to be, **life is not about the hype.**

The more I think about this idea, the more I think that it is very easy today to fall into the same trap of thinking that our life with Jesus is just about the

...the majority of our days are spent walking in the valleys of challenges and on the plains of normalcy.

3

The hype doesn't
follow us home.

hype as well. The reason I say that is because a lot of the Christian events that we go to (and that you maybe even just came home from) like concerts, conferences, festivals, camps, and even church sometimes, are filled not only with great Bible teaching, but also with pyrotechnics, laser lights and non-stop entertainment. Now, going to those events and having those experiences isn't a bad thing. In fact it's the opposite – it's a GREAT thing! I personally LOVE both going to, and speaking at, Christian music festivals, camps and other big events and seeing how **God moves in people's lives** (including my own!). Things like these are inspiring, refreshing and something all Christians should try to experience on a regular basis if at all possible. But that being said, there are some challenges we face when we leave the mountaintop and transition back to real life. They exist because when the experience is done and we go home, we don't have **fireworks** and someone leading us in passionate worship. We don't have a pumped crowd and an energetic preacher challenging us to live each day for Christ.

In other words, the hype doesn't follow us home. What does go home with us is our heart:

A heart that has hopefully been **refocused, renewed** and **restored;** a heart that has experienced the forgiveness of Christ, which has led to Jesus becoming our Savior or strengthening our existing walk with Him. The question we now face is, **How do we stay excited about our faith?** Or in other words, "How do we grow in our desire to learn more about this life in Christ each day of our normal lives?" That is a great question. And it's one that every Christ-follower, both new and old, has asked at some point or many points during his or her journey with Jesus. That's what this book, *Heart Not Hype*, is all about. It has been written to come alongside you in the new or renewed walk with Christ you are on. It has been designed so each day will only take you about 20 minutes or so to go through, but it will help you understand your relationship with Jesus better and encourage you in your faith journey.

Throughout this book, there are passages from the Bible written out for you as well as Scriptures that you are going to need to look up on your own. I encourage you to take the time to both read them when given and look them up when

How do we grow in our desire to learn more about this life in Christ each day of our normal lives?

needed. They are God's Words for you and they have **the power to transform your life** day by day.

One last thing I want to mention quickly is that just because *Heart Not Hype* is written as a 7-day book, doesn't necessarily mean you have to do to it in 7 days. Following this pace will just keep you from either being overwhelmed by all of the great info or zipping through it so quickly that you don't remember what you have read and experienced. It can also help keep you from putting it down for too long and forgetting all about it. But that being said, if you want to read more than one chapter a day or take a few days per chapter, knock yourself out. Just promise me that you will soak it in and apply it regardless of the speed you roll through it.

Okay. I'd say that's a long enough introduction. Enjoy chewing on, and digesting, *Heart Not Hype* over the next 7 days or so. And while you are doing it, always remember that at the end of the day, our walk with Christ is not about the hype – **it's about the heart.**▪ ▬ ▬ ▬ ▬ ▬ ▬ ▬

> Our walk with Christ is not about the hype – it's about the heart.

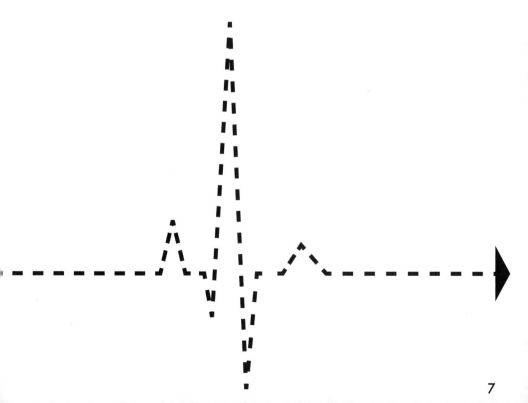

7

it's all about
relationship

I am so glad you are reading this today.
Chances are that you are holding this book
in your hand because you have either given
your life to Christ for the first time OR you have
re-committed your heart to Christ after you've
allowed yourself to lose focus for a little while.
In either case - **congratulations!**

The decision you made not only has an impact on this life but on what comes later – long after we are gone from this planet.

Often times when you hear the word
"congratulations" it is because you won some
sort of a contest, you got married, you had a
baby or you got a new job. You know, **really
important, life-altering stuff.** But in this case,
"congratulations" means so much more because
the decision you made not only has an impact
on this life but on what comes later – long after
we take our last breath.

The reason I say later is because your decision
to follow Jesus and put Him in charge of your
life means you have been adopted into God's
family (more on that later) and get to spend all
of eternity in Heaven with the One who created
you. So that being said,

CONGRATULATIONS!

And yes, the "bigness" of your decision is worthy of all caps and large print.

Now that you have begun your journey with Jesus as your Savior, what's next? I mean, what does that mean exactly? How does this decision change things for you? (Which it does, a lot.) How does this choice impact your daily life? (Quite a bit.) Are you supposed to

look **differently,**
act **differently** and
look AT things **differently?** (In a way, yes.)

Those are some good questions you may be asking yourself, but before we get into all of that, let's recap why we are even talking about all these things.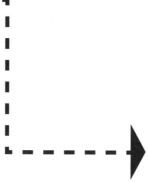

Now that you have begun your journey with Jesus as your Savior, what's next?

1

Most likely you heard some sort of sermon or message or you read something that had this kind of information in it:

God, the One who created everything, loves you and **God created you for a relationship with Him** (Genesis 1 and 2 tells us all about this).

2

There is a problem though. We have sin in our lives – all of us (Romans 3:23) – and this sin (things that we do and think that are against God's plan) separates us from God. And because God is Holy (100% pure and perfect), in order for us (people who are unholy) to be in His presence and have a relationship with Him, our sin must be forgiven and separated from us. How does that happen? Through a sacrifice of something that is pure and blameless. **This is where Jesus comes in.**

3

Prior to Jesus, God's son who was both fully God and fully man, being born on earth, God provided certain animals, like lambs, to sacrifice on an altar as a payment for the sin in people's lives. This was pretty messy, but it worked, and "got us by" until God sent His son Jesus to walk the earth for 33 years or so, healing people, performing miracles and changing the way people looked at religion. Then, at the end of those years, **Jesus became the ultimate sacrifice** and was nailed to a cross, spilling His blood as a payment for the sin of the world.

The amazing thing about this was that ALL sin, including yours and mine, was heaped on Jesus and was nailed to the cross with Him.

In other words, **Jesus took the punishment in our place** even though we did nothing to deserve it and could do nothing to earn it (Romans 5:8). How awesome is that?!

But this is not **The End.**

4

There's more to the story.

Three days after Jesus was placed in the tomb, God raised Him from the dead. What that means is that Jesus defeated death and because of that, our sin can be forgiven and we can have a relationship with God and spend all of our life, both here on this earth and in Heaven, with Him.

5

Now that, my friend, is some good stuff!

You see, what Jesus did was take "Religion" and turn it into a "Relationship." And that is what this whole "New Life in Christ" is all about – **Relationship.**

Throughout these next few days, we are going to be downloading tons of information about the Christian life into your mind and heart, but the main thing to remember is this: **It's all about relationship!**

Because of that, we'll look at how we can keep our relationship with God growing so we become more and more like Christ in every aspect of our lives, and reflect who Jesus is to all those around us.

This may seem like a big task, but don't allow yourself to get stressed out. A growing relationship with Christ is a journey that we all continuously travel. None of us have "arrived" and none of us will until we are all in Heaven together. The most important thing you can do right now is **keep focused on Jesus** and allow Him to help you learn and grow.

> What Jesus did was take "Religion" and turn it into a "Relationship."

14

I also encourage you to find someone else that you can talk about some of this stuff with. Maybe it's a pastor, a parent, a close friend or a coach – whoever would encourage you as you take these **first steps, new steps or next steps** in your relationship with God.

All right, that is it for today but again – **CONGRATULATIONS!** I am excited to be walking through all of this with you. Until we get back together tomorrow, here are a few questions for you to think and journal about.

A growing relationship with Christ is a journey that we all continuously travel.

Use the space on these pages to write, sketch and process the things that you're learning and thinking about.

How did you know it
was time to commit
your life to Christ?

1

What kind of
difference do you
want this to make in
your life?

2

Is there any part of this new "Jesus is in my life" thing that scares you or that you are nervous about?

Who is someone
that you can talk to
and journey with as
you begin this new
Christian life?

What are some things
that you'd like to ask
them about?

4

What will be (or has been) the response from family/friends etc. regarding your new relationship with Christ?

5

developing
our relationship with
Jesus

Welcome to Day 2 - I am so glad you are joining me again. I hope you took a little time to think more about the content we discussed yesterday and you are ready to dig a touch deeper today.

How do we develop a relationship with a God whom we can't even see?

Yesterday, the main idea was that this whole new **life is about a "Journey with Jesus."** And the journey is all about what? Relationship. Exactly!

So knowing relationship is key, the question that we are now faced with today is this: "How do we develop a relationship with a God whom we can't even see?" That is a great question. And the answer is the same as how you develop any relationship – TIME. I know that's probably not the earth-shattering answer that you were looking for, but it's the truth. Getting to know Jesus is just like getting to know any other friend, the more time you spend with them, the better you get to know them.

One of the greatest ways to spend your time learning more about God and what He wants to do in your life is by reading the Bible. The

Bible is **God's inspired Word** – which means
He inspired the Bible's authors with the words
they were supposed to write. Because of that,
everything in the Bible is completely true and
useful for teaching us and growing us closer to
God (2 Timothy 3:16-17).

The Bible walks us through every aspect of our
faith including one of the most foundational and
popular scriptures in the whole book, John 3:16:

> For God so loved the world that He
> gave His only Son, that whoever
> believes in Him should not perish but
> have eternal life. *(ESV)*

Take a few minutes and memorize this verse.
That way you can say it throughout the week
and really begin to believe it. Verses like this can
help us get through life – especially during
the times when it is crazy and feels like it is out of control.

> The Bible walks
> us through every
> aspect of our faith.

We were never
created for this
earth to be the
end of our story.

Got it memorized? Good job. I think that scripture verse is super-encouraging for each one of us. Because of your new or renewed faith in Jesus Christ and your decision to make Him Lord, you will now live with Him forever in Heaven. And get this – that is what you were created for. We were never created for this earth to be the end of our story.

Did you know that? It's true, we were actually **created** to spend eternity with Jesus, both here on earth and ultimately in Heaven.

That is why in Ecclesiastes 3:11 we are told that when we were created, God "put eternity into man's heart..." (ESV)

1 Peter 2:11 backs this thought up as well. It states:

> Dear friends, I warn you as temporary residents and foreigners to keep away from worldly desires that wage against your very souls... (NLT)

See? This earth isn't going to be our home forever!

Important truths like that are found throughout the entire Bible. That is why it is so important for us, as followers of Christ, to be reading the Bible as much as we can. Reading God's Word will help you understand how you can live this life, being the "New Creation" you now are because of the decision you made to make Jesus the Lord of your life.

2 Corinthians 5:17 says:

> Therefore, if anyone is in Christ, he is a new creation; the old has passed away; behold, the new has come. (ESV)

What this means is that there is a "new normal" – a new pattern – for your life. Because of your relationship with Christ, God has new things in store for you and that includes reading His Word and getting to know Him better.

So all that being said, you are probably now asking many questions, such as, "Where in the world do I start? I mean the Bible is a BIG book! And also, which one do I read? Seriously, there

Reading God's Word will help you understand how you can live this life.

are SO many versions. There's the NIV, NLT, NKJV, NIV, NSV, Women's Devotional Bible, Teen Study Bible, Children's Adventure Bible, Underwater Mammal Bible, etc. C'mon, which one do I pick?"

Seriously, there are SO many versions of the Bible – which one do I pick?

Well the truth is that any and all of them will work, because they are all God's Word; however, I would find the one that is easiest for you to understand. I personally like the New Living Translation (NLT), the New International Version (NIV) or the English Standard Version (ESV) because they are written in a language that is a little easier to relate to.

If possible, a study version would be great for you to use because many passages of scripture are explained further in the margins or at the bottom of the page so you can understand what was going on at the time it was written and relate it to today. After you pick a version of the Bible that you want to dive into, you'll want to find the table of contents at the beginning.

Once there, you will see that the Bible contains **66 books divided into 2 parts:**

The Old Testament and The New Testament.

The Old Testament (OT) is full of stories about the creation of the world, the faithfulness of God throughout the generations and everything that happened prior to Jesus coming to the earth.

The New Testament (NT) tells us how Jesus came to the earth as a baby, lived amongst and ministered to the people and then died for our sins. It also shares about the earliest followers of Christ and how we can walk closely with Christ today.

Both parts of the Bible are important to our lives as Christians.

Both parts of the Bible are important to our lives as Christians but I think that it's better for new Christians to start in the NT so you can get an understanding of God's love for you, who Christ is and how you are to live in the power of the Holy Spirit.

(The Trinity – God the Father, Jesus the Son, and the Holy Spirit – will be covered tomorrow.)

Which book should I read first?

Once you have selected a version of the Bible you are comfortable with and have decided that you will begin in the New Testament, you may ask, "Which book should I read first?" **Another good question.** Any of the first 4 books (these are referred to as the Gospels) would be great to start with but most often people start in the book of John. This book lays out Jesus' life, His ministry and His death very well. The other 3 Gospels (Matthew, Mark and Luke) are great as well and also cover His birth, teachings and death so feel free to look through those if you'd like too.

Each book of the Bible is made up of chapters (the big, bold numbers) and verses (the small numbers). **How much you read in one sitting is really up to you.** Some of you may read just a few verses and that will be enough, others may read a whole chapter or two. The point is not about HOW MUCH you are reading but that you are consistent in digging into the Bible every day and are trying to understand (and apply) what you are reading. Seriously, **don't worry** about getting a ton read each day. Just read. Little by little you will begin to understand more and more. And with each passing verse and each passing day, you will find yourself becoming more and more like Christ, and living a life of worship for Him.

OK, that's enough for today. Before the day is out, grab a Bible of choice and page through the book of John. Read some verses. Seek to understand them and ask God to help you apply them to your life. Remember, don't overwhelm yourself – just read.

You will find yourself becoming more and more like Christ.

A note about technology:

There are many apps and online resources that can help you in reading the Word as well. BibleGateway.com, for example, can show you any Bible verse(s) in any version in just a few seconds. If you have a smart phone or tablet, a Bible app that has been super useful for me is one put out by LifeChurch.tv called "You Version." They have reading plans and Bible studies that you can customize to fit your needs. Whether in print or in technology, God's Word is powerful no matter how you read it–the important thing is to find a way that works for you and read.

- - ● Again, use the space on these pages to write, sketch and process the things that you're learning and thinking about.

What verses did you
read today?

What did they say?

What do you think
they mean?

How can what you
read be applied to
your life?

1

Did you read anything
that confused you?

Who can you talk
to about your Bible
readings and/or the
Bible questions you
may have?

2

What part of reading
the Bible scares you
the most (if it does)?

Trinity
training

It's time for **day number 3...** so let's get right into it!

One of the biggest movies in the late 1990's was *The Matrix*. Lots of cool special effects that hadn't been seen before, a trippy story line and crazy good intensity from the actors made this a HUGE summer hit. I know, some of you may not have even been born yet but stay with me. One of the main characters in the movie was named Trinity, played by Carrie-Anne Moss. She was beautiful, caring, purposed and mysterious – all wrapped up into one being. She protected and guided Neo (Keanu Reeves' character) and was willing to lay it all on the line to ensure that Neo could accomplish his mission.

As we begin to walk with Christ, we can have a lot of questions.

I will get back to that in a second, but many times as we begin to walk with Christ, we can have **a lot of questions.** Hopefully this book has answered a few of those questions already and will continue to answer more over the next few days. Probably one of the biggest questions most people have about Christianity is in regards to the mystery of "The Trinity" where God the Father is God, Jesus the Son is God and the Holy Spirit is God. And the mystery is because they are not separate Gods. They are all one. Truthfully, that concept is hard to understand. But even though we won't be able to fully understand it in our humanness, God can help us learn as we ask Him for help and grow in our relationship with Him.

So let's dive into the **"Mystery of the Trinity"** or in other words, "What is the Trinity?" I once heard it said that the Trinity is God's plan of salvation in action. God the Father, desiring to restore fellowship between Himself and His creation (that's us!), sent His Son Jesus, who willingly gave His life as a substitute for our sin. After defeating evil by raising His Son from the dead, God sent His Holy Spirit to live in and empower all who believe and follow Him.

Now, that sounds really good, **but what does it mean?** Let's break it down a little more using some scripture. Grab your Bible and a pen because I am going to throw some TRUTH your way and then after each statement, there will be some Scriptures for you to look up and internalize.

> God can help us learn as we ask Him for help and grow in our relationship with Him.

God the Father

God has been depicted or described in many different ways throughout the years.

God has been depicted or described in many different ways throughout the years. A lot of people see him as **the man up in the sky holding a lightning bolt,** just waiting for us to screw up so he can throw it at us and impale us through the neck.

Others see him as **a smiling old guy** with a white beard wearing a white robe and still others, because of Hollywood movies, see Him as Morgan Freeman, Whoopi Goldberg, Jim Carrey or (going WAY back) George Burns.

But what does **Scripture** say?

Take a few minutes to look these verses up:

God has always been there and He created
everything, including us.

Genesis 1:1-31

From the beginning, God desired a relationship
with us.

Genesis 1:27
Jeremiah 24:7

When He created us, He placed a longing for
eternity (with Him) in our hearts.

Ecclesiastes 3:11

God's power and wisdom are beyond our
human ability to fully understand.

Isaiah 55:8-9
Romans 11:33-36

God's love for us has no limits.

Psalm 108:4
Romans 8:35, 38-39
Ephesians 3:16-19

What does
Scripture say about
who God is?

Jesus the Son

> Jesus is so much more than the "sweet little baby lying in the manger."

Ricky Bobby, played by Will Ferrell in the movie *Talladega Nights*, liked to think of Jesus as the "sweet little baby lying in the manger" but while he was born just like you and me, **Jesus is so much more** than the little baby. He is also more than just a "co-pilot" like a popular bumper sticker says. **Scripture** tells us this about Jesus: (Again, take a minute and look these up.)

He is the image of God the Father and all things were created by Him and for Him.

Colossians 1:15-20

He died in our place so we can experience forgiveness and freedom from sin and receive the gift of eternal life.

John 3:16
Romans 5:6-8
Ephesians 1:7
Colossians 1:21-22

Jesus was the only person who was perfect and never sinned. That is why He was the perfect sacrifice for our sin.

Hebrews 2:17-18

Jesus came to give us a full and complete life.

John 10:10

Having a relationship with Jesus is the only way for us to get to God.

John 14:6

Jesus showed us how we are to live our lives.

John 13:13-17
Matthew 22:37-38

Through Christ, we can be adopted as God's children.

Ephesians 1:4-6
John 1:12-13
Galations 4:4-7

One day soon, Jesus will return for all of those who follow Him and we will be with Him forever.

John 14:2-4
1 Thessalonians 4:16-17

What does Scripture say about who Jesus is?

the Holy Spirit

Is the Holy Spirit our conscience, or goose bumps? Or something more?

Some would say that the Holy Spirit is like a conscience that helps us distinguish between right and wrong. Others think that the Holy Spirit is the thing that gives them goose bumps when they are in church.

Scripture says the following about this important, powerful member of the Trinity:

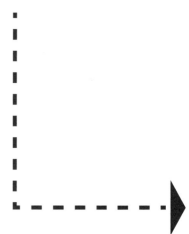

He has been a part of everything since the very beginning.

Genesis 1:2, 26

He gave Jesus the power for His earthly ministry.

Acts 10:37-38
Luke 4:14-15
Luke 5:17-25

He unites us and gives us spiritual gifts to be used for God.

1 Corinthians 12:12-13
Ephesians 4:3-6, 11-13

He is a counselor or guide that lives in us and leads us.

John 14:16-17

He keeps us from being controlled by our sinful nature.

Romans 8:9-11

He gives us power and helps us live the way we should live and accomplish what we need to do.

Acts 1:8
Matthew 28:19-20
Romans 12:1-2

How does Scripture talk about the Holy Spirit?

I know reading all of that info combined with the Scriptures was probably like drinking out of a fire hydrant, but isn't that a ton of good stuff?! Because it is so much to think about and process, I encourage you to **take some time** over the next 24 hours to slowly go over these things again and "marinate" in these Truths because they are so important to our faith and your new life. You may even need to come back to these time and time again as well just to be reminded of the awesomeness of our God.

As we wrap up for the day, I want to revisit the character Trinity, from the movie, *The Matrix*. Trinity took care of Neo. She guided him and did everything necessary in order to help him accomplish his mission. I don't think we have to stretch our imagination too far to see the similarities between her character and God the Father, Jesus the Son and the Holy Spirit. Why? Because God has done everything necessary to be with us, to take care of us and help us fulfill our mission of becoming more like Him and introducing others to Him as well!

If you ask me, I also think that *The Matrix*

> God has done everything necessary to be with us, to take care of us and help us fulfill our mission of becoming more like Him and introducing others to Him as well!

analogy further proves the point that each one of us, even those in Hollywood and the mainstream media, has eternity and their need for God **written on their hearts.** They may not know that they are searching for Christ yet, but they are. Everyone is! I don't know about you, but I am so glad that you and I have found Christ and have fulfilled that God-given need through Him!

Each one of us has eternity and our need for God written on our hearts.

The Trinity, sometimes called the "3-in-1," is a mystery beyond human understanding. Ask God to give you insight into His nature as you think about these questions.

Knowing that God
exists as the Father,
the Son and the
Holy Spirit, does that
make you feel more
confused, secure,
excited?

Why?

1

Of the Bible scriptures listed, which ones are your favorites? How come?

2

How does knowing
that God is always
with you through the
power of the Holy
Spirit, change your
view of how you go
about living each day?

3

why do we
even need a
Savior?

Why do you and I need a Savior? What do we need to be "saved" from?

So far on our *Heart Not Hype* journey, we have established that this **new life in Christ** is all about growing our relationship with Jesus and allowing Him to guide our lives through the power of the Holy Spirit. And of course **this all starts with Jesus becoming our Savior.**

So if it begins with Jesus being our Savior, that must mean that we are in need of one, right? But why? Why do you and I need a Savior? What do we need to be "saved" from? Another great question! And here's the answer - **Sin.** Do you remember talking about that in Day 1? (If you don't, or just want a refresher, feel free to flip back a few pages to the first day.)

Now, sin may be just a three-letter word, but that little word is a very big deal! Seriously, it is. In fact, like we looked at in Day 1, it is because of our sin (lying, lusting, stealing, worshipping other gods, etc.) that **Jesus had to die!** And why did He willingly die for us? Because He loves us! If Jesus hadn't died in our place, our sin could not be forgiven and there is no way we could have a relationship with Him, and spend all of eternity in Heaven like we were designed to.

Check out what it says in Romans 6:23:

> For the wages of sin is death but the
> gift of God is eternal life in Christ
> Jesus our Lord. (NIV)

So according to that Bible verse, sin is a HUGE
deal. And there isn't one person that has
ever put one foot in front of the other on this
planet except for Jesus, that is exempt from this
problem – Romans 3:23 tells us that. In other
words,

There isn't one person who is exempt from this problem, except for Jesus.

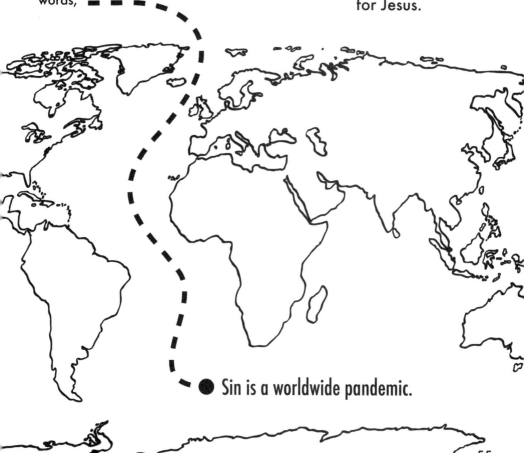

● Sin is a worldwide pandemic.

> "The thief (Satan) comes only to steal and kill and destroy..."
> John 10:10

Every year, millions of people rush out to their doctor or their local pharmacy to get their annual flu shot so they can hopefully avoid getting any of the multiple flu viruses that are out there. And why not, right? I mean, **who likes to get sick?** Nobody. Of course, getting a flu shot is just the beginning of doing what we can to stay healthy. Getting the shot doesn't mean the germs aren't still out there trying to "get us," so we also try to get plenty of sleep, take some vitamins, lather our hands in soap and maybe even cake on some sanitizer too.

All of those things are definitely good precautions to take during flu season but let me ask you this: What if we were just as concerned about sin as we are about flu germs? If our relationship with Jesus is of any importance, we will be! After all, **it is sin that separates** us from God and keeps us from growing closer in our walk with Him. And just like the germs that are out there, there is an enemy, Satan, who is prowling around like a lion ready to pounce on us (1 Peter 5:8). His whole purpose is to tempt you to sin and ruin your relationship with God. And not only that, but ruin your life. I am not being overdramatic here.

It's true! Read what John 10:10 says:

> The thief (Satan) comes only to steal
> and kill and destroy... (NIV)

See what I mean. Satan isn't messing around here. He is after us! So, what are we supposed to do? Live in fear? **Actually, no.** The first thing we need to "rest in" is the second part of John 10:10 where Jesus says:

> I have come that they (you) may
> have life, and have it to the full.
> (NIV)

"I have come that they (you) may have life, and have it to the full."

Living in fear does NOT go hand-in-hand with having "life in the full"!

Scripture also tells us that the perfect love of Jesus drives out all fear (1 John 4:18). We can take great comfort in this! The love Jesus has for us is **so much stronger** and far outweighs any fear we may have. But even though that is true, we DO need to be aware that just as Jesus and His love are real, Satan and his evil desires are real as well so be on guard. Part of 1 Peter 5:8-9 speaks to that fact: "Be alert and of sober mind...resist him (Satan) standing firm in the faith..." (NIV)

The cool thing about being told to stand firm is that God has given us some protection to do just that. It's called the **"Armor of God"** and it is found in the book of Ephesians.

> "Put on the full armor of God so that you can take your stand against the devil's schemes."
> Ephesians 6:11

Ephesians 6:10-13:

> Finally, be strong in the Lord and in His mighty power. Put on the full armor of God so that you can take your stand against the devil's schemes. For our struggle is not against flesh and blood, but against the rulers, against the authorities, against the powers of this dark world and against the spiritual forces of evil in the heavenly realms. Therefore put on the full armor of God, so that when the day of evil comes, you may be able to stand your ground, and after you have done everything, to stand. (NIV)

What Paul, the dude who wrote this book in the New Testament, is talking about here is known as spiritual warfare. Basically, what that means is that **there is a war** that is currently going on for your soul – a war between Jesus and the devil. As we have looked at throughout this book, Jesus has already done everything necessary to be with you and that makes Satan jealous and angry. Because of that, Satan is doing everything in his power (which pales in comparison to God's power, by the way) to get you away from Jesus. It's not very fun to think about, but unfortunately, it's the real deal and something that we need to remember as we live our life.

Reading God's Word will help you understand how you can live this life.

Now that we know WHY we need armor, let's take a look at the pieces of armor that the Lord has given us.

Ephesians 6:14-18a:

> Stand firm then, with the belt of truth buckled around your waist, with the breastplate of righteousness in place, and with your feet fitted with the readiness that comes from the gospel of peace. In addition to all this, take up the shield of faith, with which you can extinguish all the flaming arrows of the evil one. Take the helmet of salvation and the sword of the Spirit, which is the Word of God. And pray in the Spirit on all occasions with all kinds of prayers and requests. (NIV)

This may sound cheesy, but every morning when my kids were little, before they would head off to school, my wife and I would suit our kids up with this armor. We would act like we were putting a helmet of salvation and a belt of truth on them. We would arm them with the shield of faith and the sword of the Spirit. We

The enemy's goal is to capture our hearts and minds and destroy us.

read scripture together. We prayed over them. And we did that because the enemy's goal is to **capture** their hearts and minds and **destroy** them. And he wants to do the same to us. The armor isn't just for kids. It's for each of us. And we need to put it on every day.

Let me end with this encouragement to you: Read the Word of God! This will make you strong against the attacks of the enemy. A lot of Christians are very weak when they stare at sin and Satan in the face, and that is due in large part to their lack of time in the Scriptures. So, do yourself and your relationship with God a favor and **arm yourself with God's Word!**

See you tomorrow for a look at prayer. Here are some questions for you to think/write about in the meantime.

Read the Word of God! This will make you strong against the attacks of the enemy.

Jesus has forgiven your sin through His death and resurrection. What has been the hardest part of letting that sin go and not returning to it?

1

How have you been tempted by Satan to sin since coming into a relationship with Jesus?

What is the greatest
struggle you are
facing right now in
your relationship with
Christ?

3

After going through
the past few days with
Christ as your Savior,
what has been the best
part? How about the
hardest part?

4

How can you get better at "putting on the armor of God" each day?

5

a little (BIG) thing called

prayer

So what is it about prayer that puzzles people?

Before you get into today, let me first say that I think it is awesome that you are continuing to follow through on your commitment to grow in your walk with Christ through reading this book. Hopefully it is making at least a little difference in your life and helping you understand the plan your creator, God, has for your life.

Today, we are going to look at a very important piece in developing your relationship with God: **prayer.** Many people are confused by it, but as you will see, there really is very little to be confused about. So what is it about prayer that puzzles people? For one, a lot of people think you do the prayer thing just before meals or only while your hands are folded when you're kneeling by your bed at night. And while those may be a couple of times that prayer is often practiced, the Bible tells us something different. 1 Thessalonians 5:17 says that we should **"pray continually"** (NIV) which basically means all the time. WHAT? How in the world are we supposed to do that?

Well first of all, our perspective of what prayer is probably needs to change. Most of us are tempted to think that prayer is just when you close your eyes and start uttering **words to the sky.** That isn't necessarily wrong, but it's more than that. We need to start thinking of prayer as **communication.** It is talking with the God who created the universe, but it is still just communication. And just as communication is key to any other relationship, it is also vital in your relationship with God.

Think about it. It would be pretty hard to develop a relationship with someone if you never talked to them, right? Well, it's the same with God. If we don't have times where we both talk to, as well as listen to Him, we won't really get to know Him very well. That's why the Bible tells us to pray continually. This means that we have to start paying attention to God's blessings and look for Him wherever we are. This may seem weird when you first start doing it, but I promise that you will "see" God if you are looking – in the trees and in the rest of His creation, through other people as you talk with them, and even as you pay bills and do your homework. Yes, even then! The point is that you seek to recognize God's presence through-out the day and share **conversation** with Him.

It would be pretty hard to develop a relationship with someone if you never talked to them, right?

But what do you talk with Him about? Hmm...
how about ▬ ▬ ▪

▪ ▬ ▬ EVERYTHING?

Tell Him when you are stressed, when you're angry (even at Him) and when you are sad. You can tell him anything because He is God and He can handle it.

Seriously, I mean it. You can tell him your doubts and fears, your struggles and temptations, your joys and triumphs, and even your sorrows. You can tell Him when you are stressed, when you're angry (even at Him) and when you are sad. You can tell him anything because He is God and He can handle it. You can ask him for what you need and of course, you will want to thank Him for all the wonderful things in your life and for sticking with you during the things that haven't been so wonderful. You can tell Him how grateful you are for His love and that you love Him in return.

Here are a few scriptures for you to look up to show you what I'm talking about:

Psalm 8 – 9:2

Psalm 17:1-9

Luke 18:9-14

Philippians 4:6-7

The truth is that there really is no right or wrong way to pray.

So now that we know more about what we can pray about, **how do we do it?** To put it another way, what's the best way to pray? The truth is that there really is no right or wrong way to pray. God longs for us to communicate with Him so the importance isn't so much focused on how we pray, but that we actually engage in prayer. Sometimes this will be in the form of **"sentence prayers"** throughout the day where we thank Him with words of worship or ask Him for help. This is part of Paul's challenge to us in 1 Thessalonians to pray continuously. There will also be times though where you should take some extended time to focus on and be with the Lord.

Here are some things that you can do to help you focus during those extended times, so your mind doesn't wander or you don't fall into the temptation of falling asleep like the disciples did. (For more on that story you can check out Matthew 26:36-45)

These things will help you focus during extended prayer times with the Lord.

1 Get in **a quiet space** – The world is stinkin' loud, isn't it? Sometimes it is important to be disciplined and shut everything off (including our iPods, cell phones, TV's, Facebook, etc.) and listen to the sound of silence. It's pretty hard to hear God's voice if we are listening to our favorite band or checking out one of our 1,327 friends statuses on Facebook. So, shut those things off for a segment of your day so you can speak to and hear from the Lord.

2 In a journal or on a piece of paper write down your blessings, requests and needs – Often times, we can have the best intentions to pray, but when we finally get around to it, we can't remember what we wanted to pray about, so our mind wanders and we can barely put a sentence together.

So grab a pen, some paper or a journal and **start writing**...and then don't forget where you put that list!

3 Withdraw or leave "normal life" for a little bit – In Mark 1:35-38, Jesus gives us a great example of how we should pray and a major reason why we do it. He gets up early in the morning and **goes** to pray. What a GREAT way to start your day!

Jesus gives a great example of how we should pray.

The key word here is "GOES!" Jesus separates himself from the world so that he doesn't have anything competing with His focus for that bit of time. Where you go doesn't really matter. It can be a different room in your house, a nature trail in your community or a quiet table in the corner of a coffee shop. Wherever it is, just withdraw. Jesus did it, so we probably should too.

4 Follow a "Prayer Map" – Sometimes praying without a guideline can create frustration. That is why Jesus laid out a format called **'The Lord's Prayer'** that we too can follow. Take a minute to look that up in Matthew 6:9-13.

Another great map to follow – one I learned as a kid – is the ACTS method of prayer.

Adoration: This is where you just spend some time thanking God for who He is and for His love and acknowledging that He is God and you are not.

Confession: Admitting the things we have done wrong (sin) and asking God to forgive us is so important to do. It is a powerful thing to own up to where we have "fallen short" so we can experience freedom and forgiveness in our walk with Jesus. Confessing our sin and receiving forgiveness removes the barrier that sin creates between God and us. That is awesome!

Thanksgiving: Showing gratitude and thanking God for everything He has given you and provided for you is key to living a joyful life in Christ. Even when there are challenges you are facing, there are still many things you can be thankful for. Thanking God for the big and small blessings in your life will also keep you from focusing on the negative stuff that our world is full of.

Supplication: This is a big word that basically means 'asking.' God loves providing for your needs (and even some of your wants!) so bring your requests to Him and ask Him to "supply every need of yours according to His riches in glory in Christ Jesus." (Philippians 4:19, ESV)

Well, there you go - **Prayer 101.** Before we are done for the day though, let me just encourage you with one more thing. Don't worry about how good your prayers are or if you are praying "good enough." Remember, **there is no right way** to do it. You don't have to say all the right things in the right way or sound really spiritual when you pray. Adopt the NIKE slogan for your prayer life and JUST DO IT! Just talk to God like you would to any other friend. By doing that, your relationship with Him will grow as you both talk to, and hear from, God.

You don't have to say all the right things in the right way or sound really spiritual when you pray.

How have today's thoughts and scriptures on prayer changed and challenged you in how you view prayer?

1

Read Matthew 6:5-8

In this passage, what
is important to Jesus in
how we pray?

2

What do you think will
be the hardest part
about prayer for you
to do?

3

Is there a time in your day that you can set aside so you can withdraw, like Jesus did, on a regular basis?

4

it's time to
love

During the past five days, you have already learned and processed tons of Truth that is helping you develop your relationship with Jesus. We're not done yet though because there are still some important topics to cover.

Your journey with Jesus is just beginning.

Now before we jump into today, it's important for you to know that even after you are done reading this book in a few days, your "Journey with Jesus" will not be done. In fact, it's just the opposite. It's only the beginning! One of the goals of this experience was to help you understand the basics about your new faith in Christ and paint a picture of what you should try and do each day so your relationship with God can grow. Things that we have covered like reading your Bible, seeking to better understand the power of Holy Spirit and praying are all a part of this relationship.

In a way, *Heart Not Hype* has been helping you learn how to fly so that when you are finished reading this book and "leave the nest", you will be able to spread your wings and soar. There will still be times where you'll get weak or tired and it will seem like you are falling from the sky, but one of the beautiful things about God is that when we feel like that, He promises to catch us, renew our strength and help us along the way. Take a look at some great words from the book of Isaiah:

> Do you not know? Have you not heard? The Lord is the everlasting God, the Creator of the ends of the earth. He will not grow tired or weary, and His understanding no one can fathom. He gives strength to the weary and increases the power of the weak. Even youths grow tired and weary, and young men stumble and fall; but those who hope in the Lord will renew their strength. They will soar on wings like eagles; they will run and not grow weary, they will walk and not be faint. (Isaiah 40:28-31 NIV)

"He will not grow tired or weary, and His understanding no one can fathom. He gives strength to the weary and increases the power of the weak."
Isaiah 40:29

With that being said (or read), let me encourage you to finish these last few days of "flight training" with excitement and strength!

Today, we're going to look at two of the most **crucial spiritual disciplines** that will help you both grow in your relationship with Christ and show those around you that you have Christ in your heart.

Are you ready for them? They are big. In fact if you can catch these spiritual disciplines and apply them, you will be well on your way to becoming more and more like Jesus. Here are a couple of scriptures that are central to these important Christian values:

> An expert in the law tested Jesus with this question: Teacher, which is the greatest commandment in all the law? Jesus replied: 'Love the Lord your God with all your heart and with all your soul and with all your mind. This is the first and greatest commandment. And the second is like it: Love your neighbor as yourself.' (Matthew 22:35-39, NIV)

> For even the Son of Man came not to be served but to serve others and to give his life as a ransom for many. (Matthew 20:28, NLT)

We were never created for this earth to be the end of our story.

Any guesses as to what the focus is today?
Yep...you got it: **Loving** and **Serving.**

Friends, when we love and serve other people, two things happen:

1 We grow in Christ because we are doing what Jesus himself did: Loving people and serving them. So when we do that (love and serve), we are becoming like Christ – which is exactly what God wants for our lives!

2 Others are drawn to Christ. Why are other people drawn to the person of Jesus? It's the same answer as above: Because we are doing what Jesus himself did – loving people and serving them.

One of the biggest hindrances in our "Jesus Journey" is when we forget that life is not spent with our nose buried in the Bible, our head bowed in prayer or just sitting in a church pew or chair on Sunday mornings. I am NOT discounting those things AT ALL, especially since we just spent the last few days looking at the importance of them. BUT, those things are only

> One of the biggest hindrances in our "Journey with Jesus" is when we forget that life is not spent with our nose buried in the Bible, our head bowed in prayer or just sitting in a church pew or chair on Sunday mornings.

the beginning. Those practices are to prepare us to live our lives in love and service to God and to others. Check out 1 Corinthians 13:2:

> If I had the gift of prophecy, and if I understood all of God's secret plans and possessed all knowledge, and if I had such faith that I could move mountains, but didn't love others, I would be nothing. (NLT)

We MUST understand that "living without loving" isn't an option in the eyes of the Lord.

If I don't love others, I am nothing. Wow! Isn't that kind of harsh? Well, loving people is **a pretty big deal** to God. After all, it was because of love for us and for others that He sent Jesus to the cross to die for us. (For another great scripture, take a look at 1 John 3:16.) This means we MUST understand that "living without loving" isn't an option in the eyes of the Lord. Unfortunately, it's a reality that many Christ followers find themselves in. Yeah, maybe they ARE devoted to God and living for Him, but if they do not love others (and that means ALL others) then that is **a major problem.** So much so that Jesus says this in Matthew 7:21:

> Not everyone who says to me,
> 'Lord, Lord,' will enter the kingdom

of heaven, but only the one who
does the will of my Father who is in
heaven. (NIV)

Loving people, even the unlovable ones, is part of
God's will for our lives. Don't worry if this doesn't
come naturally right away. This is something that
you will get better and better at the longer you
are walking with the Lord. The key is being aware
of this so you can work on it. Loving people the
way Jesus loved us is also important because
that is what separates Christianity from the rest of
the world's religions and what will prompt us to
care for others and their needs. This places in us a
desire to share Christ's love with them. Take a look
at 1 John 4:7-12:

Loving people,
even the unlovable
ones, is part of
God's will for our
lives.

> Dear friends, let us continue to love
> one another, for love comes from
> God. Anyone who loves is a child
> of God and knows God. But anyone
> who does not love does not know
> God, for God is love. God showed
> how much he loved us by sending
> his one and only Son into the world
> so that we might have eternal life
> through him. This is real love—not

God's love in us should propel us to love others and show that love in tangible ways.

that we loved God, but that he loved us and sent His Son as a sacrifice to take away our sins. Dear friends, since God loved us that much, we surely ought to love each other. No one has ever seen God. But if we love each other, God lives in us, and His love is brought to full expression in us. (NLT)

The full expression of God's love in us should propel us to **love others** and show that love in tangible ways. In John 13, Jesus shows love to His followers in a crazy way – He washes their feet! That may not seem like that big of a deal, but in those days, everyone wore sandals and they walked everywhere. This meant that those dudes' feet were stinky, sweaty and dirty. Seriously. Not just a little dusty. I'm talkin' DIRTY. And Jesus, the King the Kings, the Savior of the world humbled Himself and washed 12 pairs of dirty feet. He did this out of love. He did this out of humility. He did this as an example. **Jesus showed his disciples (and us) what it is to love and serve other people.**

Jesus ends this experience by saying in verses 15-17 of John chapter 13:

> I have set you an example that you should do as I have done for you. Very truly I tell you, no servant is greater than his master, nor is a messenger greater than the one who sent him. Now that you know these things, you will be blessed if you do them. (NIV)

Some of the greatest times of growth in our lives come when we stop focusing on ourselves and seek out opportunities to **love** and **serve** other people in the name of Jesus.

We don't necessarily do this because we want to feel good about ourselves, although that probably will happen, but we do it because we want to be obedient to God and show the same kind of love that we have experienced in our lives. So with that, here is **a final challenge** for you:

Love and serve God with all that you are and love and serve others in the same way.

Love and serve God with all that you are and love and serve others in the same way.

Would you say that it is easy or difficult for you to love others? Why?

1

When you think about
serving others, does
that give you joy or is
it more of a chore?

2

How does knowing
how much Jesus loves
you change your
perspective on how
we are to love others?

3

In thinking about
serving in the name
of Jesus, how can you
serve someone this
week that will show
Christ's love?

4

double-comm

(community and commission)

Hey guess what? You made it to day 7. Congratulations on sticking with *Heart Not Hype* the whole week. Before we wrap this all up, we need to look at just a couple more things that are important to your continual growth and journey with Christ: Community and Commission.

First, lets tackle community. Today, I want to encourage you to think about churches that are in your community or city. Now with a few of those in mind, do you know anyone that is going to one of them? Maybe a friend or a relative? Possibly a neighbor? A former good-looking baby sitter? Ok, maybe that one isn't a very good idea.

Anyway, the reason I ask is because it is super important for you to plug into a local church so you can connect with others that are on this same journey with Jesus that you are. Now, I know that right now some of you are thinking that church is going to be boring, stuffy and full of people that will just look at you like you are some kind of freak that doesn't belong. And I am not going to lie to you. You may feel like

> It is super important for you to plug into a local church so you can connect with others that are on this same journey with Jesus that you are.

that at a church or two. But keep searching until you find one that teaches the Bible in a way you can understand and apply it, as well as one that feels like home. That may sound crazy, but when you find the right church, you'll know it. Even if the rest of the people there don't look like you, still try to get connected, because just as we talked about from the very beginning,

you are not meant to walk this path alone.

Your relationship with Jesus is a personal one for sure, but it is definitely not private! Believe me, you will be both stronger in your walk with God and feel encouraged when you are connected to a church. This isn't just me saying it either. Scripture tells us the same thing. Check it:

> **Keep searching until you find one that teaches the Bible in a way you can understand and apply it, as well as one that feels like "home."**

Let us think of ways to motivate one another to acts of love and good works. And let us not neglect our meeting together, as some people do, but encourage one another, especially now that the day of his return is drawing near. (Hebrews 10:24-25, NLT)

Being a part of a church community through

things like worship services, youth groups and/or small groups is vital to you. It will be a lifeline to something that will keep you growing and thriving. It will encourage and strengthen you when trials and temptations come your way.

As you are looking for a church, remember – just as there are no perfect people, there is no perfect church.

In Acts 2:42-47, Luke (the writer) paints a picture of what the church is to be:

> They devoted themselves to the apostles' teaching and to fellowship, to the breaking of bread and to prayer. Everyone was filled with awe at the many wonders and signs performed by the apostles. All the believers were together and had everything in common. They sold property and possessions to give to anyone who had need. Every day they continued to meet together in the temple courts. They broke bread in their homes and ate together with glad and sincere hearts, praising God and enjoying the favor of all the people. And the Lord added to their number daily those who were being saved. (NIV)

What a beautiful portrait of what the Body of Christ is supposed to be like. But, there is one thing you NEED to remember as you are looking for a church: just as there are no perfect people, there is no perfect church. Trying to find the right church may prove to be difficult at first but it is one of the most important things you can do as you walk with Jesus. So give it some time. Check some out and find out where you can learn more about Christ, serve like Jesus did and have true fellowship and friendship with others.

You now have a story about how you came to know Christ and the difference He has made in your life.

Now onto the second big word of the day –
Commission. The last line of that passage we just looked at is, "And the Lord added to their number daily those who were being saved." The best thing about that verse is this: you have a part in that! It's true.

Because you have come to know Christ as your Savior and you are now walking with Him, you now have what is known as a testimony, which is really just a fancy word for a story about how you came to know Christ and the difference He has made in your life. The cool thing about having a testimony is that Jesus now wants you to join Him in His work and to share it (your story) with others. Radical idea, eh? So radical, in fact, that this is the very last idea (actually it was more of **a mandate** or an order), that Jesus gives His followers before he goes up to Heaven where He is now preparing a place for you and me. He said this in the book of Matthew:

Jesus wants you to join Him in His work and to share your story with others.

> Therefore go and make disciples of all nations, baptizing them in the name of the Father and of the Son and of the Holy Spirit, and teaching them to obey everything I have commanded you. And surely I am with you always, to the very end of the age.
> (Matthew 28:19-20 NIV)

The gospel of Mark puts it this way:

> Go into all the world and preach the Good News to everyone.
> (Mark 16:15 NLT)

That my friend, is called '**The Great Commission**' and it is for each one of us to join in. Now, most of us are not professional speakers that want to get up and share our story to thousands, hundreds or maybe even tens of people. But here's the deal: no one else has your story of how you met Christ and what He has done for you. So if you don't share it, **who will?** In those verses, Jesus is basically saying to you, "You need to share your story!" By doing that, **you will bring glory to God** and you will be following God's plan. I love this!

So now you're probably saying, "Alright, I get it. I am supposed to share my story but what am I supposed to say?" Well, let me make this really easy for you. You don't have to say that much. **Really.** Here is a simple breakdown of how this could look for you:

1. How you were before you met Christ. (1 minute)

2. How you met Christ. (1 minute)

3. How Christ has made a difference in your life. (3 minutes)

Maybe it won't take you five minutes to get through your story but the important thing is that

> No one else has your story of how you met Christ and what He has done for you. If you don't share it, who will?

Let's "give it all we've got" and see what we can accomplish for God and the growth of His Kingdom!

you share how Jesus has forgiven you of your sins and how He has transformed your life. And God wants you to do that with as many people as possible. Of course it is crucial that your LIFE backs up your story, so make sure that you are walking the walk and not just talking the talk. It wouldn't make much sense if you said one thing and did another, right? We all know people that are like that and usually we don't choose to hang out with or even trust them. So let's make sure that we do all we can to make sure our words match up with our lifestyle. We don't have to be perfect because God's grace and forgiveness covers us when we struggle, so let's "give it all we've got" and see what we can accomplish for God and the growth of His Kingdom!

It's fun to think about how many people you could possibly lead to Christ because of first saying "yes" to Him yourself. Don't be intimidated by this. A good way to start is by listing three to five people you currently know and start praying for them. Then ask God for opportunities to share the Good News of Jesus with them. In fact, why don't you take a few minutes right now and ask God for the names of

five people in your world who need Christ and
then list them below:

1

2

3

4

5

Now that you have this list made, I encourage
you to spend some time praying for them,
by name, each day and asking the Lord
for the ability to influence them for Him. I
also encourage you to **dream big** and not
underestimate the impact you could have for
the Lord. His plans are HUGE for your life, so
step out and get involved in the growth of His
Kingdom. Walk across the street, start a Bible
study in your school, talk with someone at the
office, go on a mission trip. Whatever you do,
get active! There are way too many people
who don't know Jesus to just sit around and
keep the Good News to yourself.

There are way too
many people who
don't know Jesus to
just sit around and
keep the Good
News to yourself.

As you think about churches in your area, does anybody you know go to one of them? If so, could you and maybe even your family tag along with them this Sunday? If not, is there a church that you would be interested in checking out?

1

Is there anything that would keep you from going to church this Sunday? If so, what is it?

2

When thinking about sharing your new faith and your story with others, does that make you excited or nervous? If you are fearful, how can you overcome that fear?

3

Who is somebody that you know pretty well that you could share your new faith with and help you overcome the challenge of sharing it for the first time?

4

Final thoughts

Well my friend, **congratulations** again for deciding to follow Jesus and great job on sticking with this 7-Day Journey. Always remember that discipleship and our journey with Christ is a life-long adventure that is about the HEART, not the HYPE. There will be great times ahead and there will be some challenging ones. The important thing is that no matter what kind of season of life you go through in the future, good and/or difficult, stay in God's Word, keep praying and enjoy fellowship with other believers. I also encourage you to come back to these studies in the future to remind yourself of the things that God has done for you and why your commitment to Christ is the most important decision you have ever made. It can also continue to provide encouragement for you along the way. Feel free to tell others about *Heart Not Hype* as well. Maybe it can help them in their journey.

Finally, as we close, I want you to know that I am super proud of you, and more importantly, God is. Keep your eyes on Him and He will keep your path straight (Proverbs 3:5-6). I pray His richest blessings and supernatural presence for each day of your life. See you in Heaven, if not before.

* I would love to hear more about your story, how Heart Not Hype helped you in your walk with Jesus or anything else you'd like to share. You can email your thoughts, prayer requests and stories to heartnothype@resgen.org. You can also connect with us on the Restoration Generation Facebook page or find me on Twitter: @tchenderson, #heartnothype.

resgen.org

About the author

Tom Henderson is the founder and lead
communicator for Restoration Generation
(resgen.org, resgenschools.org). He is driven by
a passion to reach people with the life-saving
message of Jesus Christ and help them restore
the broken relationships in their lives. He is a
16-year youth ministry veteran, a graduate of
the University of Sioux Falls, an ambassador for
Compassion International and a member of Luis
Palau's Next Generation Alliance of Evangelists.
He speaks to crowds ranging from 50 to 50,000
at festivals, camps, conferences, schools and
other events throughout the country.

Tom Henderson
Restoration Generation
tomh@resgen.org
@tchenderson
resgen.org

Tom has been married to
Laura for over 16 years,
and has 2 boys, Isaiah
and Chase, both of whom
he coaches in baseball
and various lawn games
like bean bag and bocce ball. When he's not
speaking on the road, Tom volunteers as a youth
leader at his local church, Central Baptist, in
Sioux Falls, SD.

Invite Tom to Speak
To inquire about Tom
speaking at your
event, festival or
school, send an email
to tomh@resgen.org
or visit resgen.org for
scheduling/booking
information.

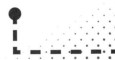

Responses to
Heart Not Hype

Partial rescues aren't really rescues at all. That's why giving a boat to someone lost at sea isn't enough. They also need other crucial resources such as a compass, food, water and a chart. Tom Henderson's *Heart Not Hype* takes spiritual rescue beyond just a boat! This book is a complete survival pack for those who've been pulled out of the sea of sin. Each page gives them vital resources to help them navigate their way into the abundant life.

Tony Nolan, speaker and author;
Co-founder of TNT Ministries

This book is rock solid and should be read by every person coming to faith! It is substance that anyone desiring to be a disciple should read. It's the basics and yet deep meat at the same time. Buy it for your kids. Buy it for your youth group. Buy it for yourself! A great mix of the Word of God, stories and of course, application!

Bob Lenz, speaker and author;
Founder and President, Life Promotions and Lifest

Ever since the Lord led us to start the Creation Festival in 1979, the greatest joy continues to be seeing thousands of people streaming to the prayer tent to give their lives to Christ. Each of them then needs to grow in their new-found faith to face the real world outside of the festival grounds. Tom Henderson, in *Heart Not Hype,* has written an easy to read, 7-step, interactive devotional that takes the new Believer into a deeper understanding of what has transpired. They will be encouraged to dig deeper in discovering God and His salvation, His Word and being His servant. This book is an excellent bridge to move a person from the genuine passion of the moment to establishing a strong foundation for future growth.

Rev. Dr. Harry L. Thomas, Jr.

Director and Co-Founder, Creation Festivals

For those of us on the front-lines of youth work this book is long overdue, Tom breaks the Christian journey down into digestible chunks and reminds us all why we should love Jesus and live 100% for Him. I recommend this book to anyone working with students desiring a plumb-line to share the meaningful truths in impactful ways. Students will not only enjoy the read, but more importantly, gain a passion to live it.

Jason Folkerts, Youth Pastor

25-year youth ministry veteran

Tom is creative, engaging and relevant in his public speaking and he demonstrates the same qualities in his writing. This book provides an excellent resource to assist new believers in taking their critical next steps and developing a foundation for the greatest adventure a human heart can go on – the life-long journey of faith in Jesus Christ!

Jon Hauser, founding pastor, Prairie Heights Comm.

Church, Fargo, ND;

leadership speaker/trainer/coach, John Maxwell Team

In this straight forward, easy to read book, Tom covers all the basics of the beginning steps of a relationship with Jesus. It's an incredible resource for students, or anyone, who has just started their walk with Christ...and it's a great refresher for those who've already been on their journey for a while.

Dan Larson, Director of Young Life, Pueblo, CO

26-year youth ministry professional

Heart Not Hype is the type of book that we want every First Priority student to have their hands on as they return home from camps, retreats, events and outreach trips throughout the year. It is clear, concise and provides tangible steps for youth to take, to increase their walk with The Lord throughout their junior/high school years.

Steve Cherrico, Executive Director
First Priority Nashville

Many follow up tools have been designed for the new Christian, but too often they fall short either by being overly complex or being inadequately shallow. *Heart not Hype* strikes a good balance between simplicity and depth. Tom maintains this balance primarily by his style of communication and strategy of design. He carefully provides conceptual connections that give the participant easy access to the basics of complex ideas like the Trinity, Christ's atonement, and the authority of Scripture. At the same time he thoroughly explains the "how tos" for Bible reading, prayer, participating in a community of faith, loving God, loving others and sharing one's story of God's saving work with others. In *Heart Not Hype* the Christian community has been given an excellent tool to help new believers with the basics of their relationship with Jesus.

Rev. Chris May, Senior Pastor
South Salem (OR) Church of the Nazarene